Cat Haiku

Cat Haiku

Deborah Coates

WITH ILLUSTRATIONS BY
SANDRA BRUCE

arrow books

Published by Arrow Books in 2003

1 3 5 7 9 10 8 6 4 2

First published in the United Kingdom in 2001 by Century

Arrow Books Limited
The Random House Group Limited
20 Vauxhall Bridge Road, London SW1V 2SA

Random House Australia (Pty) Limited
20 Alfred Street, Milsons Point, Sydney,
New South Wales 2061, Australia

Random House New Zealand Limited
18 Poland Road, Glenfield,
Auckland 10, New Zealand

Random House South Africa (Pty) Limited
Endulini, 5a Jubilee Road,
Parktown 2193, South Africa

The Random House Group Limited Reg. No. 954009
www.randomhouse.co.uk

A CIP catalogue record for this book
is available from the British Library

Papers used by Random House UK Limited are natural, recyclable products
made from wood grown in sustainable forests. The manufacturing processes
conform to the environmental regulations of the country of origin.

ISBN 0 09 946328 8

Typeset in Bodoni Book

Design by Roger Walker

Printed and bound in Denmark by Nørhaven Book, Viborg

For Quinn

the best godson in the world

Acknowledgements

My heartfelt thanks to:

. . . Sharon Gedan, who over the years has helped me put the pieces together more times than either of us probably wants to think about;

. . . my parents, who instilled in me a love of books so profound that I'm still amazed I stopped reading long enough to write one of my own;

. . . Jackie Matosian, who gave me the idea for *Cat Haiku*;

. . . my agent, Todd Keithley, and editor, Amy Einhorn, whose enthusiasm, interest, patience, and support made the mysteries of first-time book publication a joy;

. . . and most of all, my grandmother, who taught me how to laugh at life, and at myself.

I owe an enormous debt to you all.

Contents

Introduction

Some of you more inquisitive types are bound to ask, 'Why write a book of cat haiku?'

Good question. My thoughtful, reasoned response as a woman of letters is . . . I have no idea. It just sort of happened – probably because I like cats, and I also like haiku (and haiku, by the way, for those of you who don't know, is a three-line, unrhymed Japanese verse form of five, seven, and five syllables respectively. So there).

Really, though, I suppose I wrote *Cat Haiku* because cats seem to think – and even communicate – in a haiku-like fashion. And that's intriguing, and often funny:

> Oh, good. You're home. I
> Celebrate joyously with
> A rousing ear-twitch.

See what I mean? Cats are, simply, the animal embodiment of haiku. Both are subtle, elegant, succinct; every nuance is fraught with meaning (however obscure that meaning may sometimes be, and believe me, it frequently is). You pay attention when you read haiku because you don't want to miss anything, and you pay attention when cats are around because you don't want to miss anything, either. There's no skimming with either one. (And if there is, especially with the latter, woe betide you.)

Also, both cats and haiku have staying power. Domestic cats have been around since the heyday of Ancient Egypt, and haiku dates from the seventeenth century or thereabouts.

I mean, we're talking *classics* here.

And who can argue with that?

Socializing

You may call it 'a
Lot of yowling'. *I* call it
Singing to my friends.

* * *

A cat friend visits.
I swat him anyway, just
For principle's sake.

I think that the new
Kitten makes a fine punching
Bag and trampoline

* * *

You are my best friend,
Person Allergic to Cats.
Let me shed on you.

I grope under the
Door with a splayed paw; I know
You're in there. Come out!

$*\quad*\quad*$

We meet outside; I
Startle. You're out of context;
Go back inside, please!

Visitors come. They
Coo over me. Ignoring
Them, I wash my rump.

* * *

Your friends seem nice: calm,
Attentive and kind. So when
Are they going home?

I hide under the
Bed. I don't want to be friends.
Take that child away!

*   *   *

There will be canine
Parts missing if that dog gets
Anywhere near me.

You want to cuddle;
I don't. No offence meant, but
Right now you bore me.

* * *

I yowl to the moon;
I am king of the night. Hear
Me and weep, Fluffy.

Recreation

Look at it from my
Perspective: clean laundry is
Meant for prowling in.

* * *

Surprise! I can jump
Through the newspaper while you
Are still reading it!

On safari, I
Prowl old shoes and sporting goods
In our junk closet.

*　*　*

Fresh catnip's no fun.
Now, some extremely dead mole –
That's good to roll in!

Paper clips, coins, an
Ice cube, you name it. I can
Slapshoot *anything*.

*   *   *

This ball is boring.
But if you had brought me a
Nice small frightened bird . . . !

Styrofoam peanuts:
To you, packaging. To me,
Rodent substitutes.

*   *   *

Those little toy mice
Are dumb; bring me an injured
Lizard or something.

To you, a water-
Filled sink. To me, a fish pond.
It just takes vision.

*   *   *

Velcro-tab sneakers
Are dull. Shoelaces, now – *those*
Are fascinating.

Home
Decorating

Is it not lovely
The way my fur wafts through the
Air when you pet me?

* * *

Au contraire; I think
The couch looks better with a
Few shredded cushions

I disagree with
You. I think cat hair dresses
The place up nicely.

* * *

I can't help it if
The curtain rod is not strong
Enough to hold me.

So I have done some
Flower arranging. *I* need
Roughage, too, you know.

*   *   *

I know you're mad, but
Just think: it takes planning to
Knock over a chair!

I leave sharp kibble
Bits where you'll step on them with
Your tender bare feet.

* * *

Voilà: grey paw prints
On the countertops. What an
Artistic statement!

Lamps are convenient
For trapping moths, but they *do*
Tip over a lot.

*   *   *

The scrunched-up throw rugs
Add a nice casual touch
Of welcome, don't they?

I fix one thing, you
Change it back. I just can't keep
Things nice around here.

Keeping Fit

I am a strong and
Adventurous cat. So I
Can't climb down. Big deal.

* * *

It's hard to explain:
Bare toes look just like small pink
Mice. Ergo, I pounce.

I leap for a bird
And miss. I pretend I was
Stretching, to fool you.

* * *

You don't get it: a
Scratching post is too easy.
Now, a chair leg – ah!

I'm not digging in
The carpet; I'm exploring
My Inner Kitten.

*　*　*

I stretch forward, then
Scrunch back. Pointing my paws is
Simply good form. See?

Studies have shown that
It is much easier to
Climb walls by moonlight.

*　*　*

It's hard to drink out
Of the toilet, but it's a
Personal challenge.

Bif! Crash! I bounce off
The walls. I'm not crazy, I'm
Self-actualized.

Food and Drink

Warning: I can't be
Trusted if fresh sushi is
Left unattended.

*   *   *

If this stuff is so
'Good and nutritious', why
Don't *you* eat kibble?

You don't understand.
The water in the toilet
Tastes a LOT better.

*   *   *

How would you like it
If *your* food was dried into
Hard little brown bits?

If I were fed an
Occasional salad, I
Would *never* eat grass.

*   *   *

Hasn't anyone
Around here ever heard of
Something called *wet* food?

You like ethnic food,
So why shouldn't *I* sneak the
Dog's food when I can?

* * *

I'm not sure what this
Was when it was alive, but
Isn't it nice now?

You say chocolate
Is bad for cats, but I think
You are just greedy.

Under the
Weather

Now we know: I should
Not eat sardines even if
It *is* my birthday.

* * *

I would have thought you'd
Thank me for getting sick where
You could not see it.

Poinck! I spit out the
Pill underneath the stove and
Watch you fish for it.

* * *

My stomach revolts:
A leaf, saliva, grass. A
Feline sushi plate.

It takes practice to
Sneeze medicine in your face.
I'm good at it, huh?

* * *

Driving to the vet
I MUST crouch underneath this
Nice safe gas pedal

A truth we both know:
The cat carrier is not
'A fun place to play'!

* * *

You went away; I
Stayed at the vet's. Why should I
Acknowledge you now?

If the vet took *your*
Temperature that way, I
Bet you'd complain, too.

Personal Issues

Eyes closed, I lick and
Lick my fur. One gets into
The Zen of it all.

* * *

I wait for you to
Clean the rugs. Hack! Hack! Here: my
Best hairball to date.

You are wrong. There's no
Rule that says the litter must
Stay *inside* the box.

*   *   *

I like to pick at
My feet with my teeth, it's a
Cat thing. Let it go.

Yes, actually,
I *am* burying a moose
In the litter box!

* * *

Oops: another hair
Ball. Sorry; guess I'm having
A bad hair ball day.

I don't make you lick
Yourself, so why must I be
Bathed with flea shampoo?

Repose

Sometimes my front legs
Keep walking while my back legs
Decide to lie down.

*   *   *

It's true: cats always
Know the most comfortable
Place. But you won't fit.

I don't like my bed.
I prefer your favourite
Chair. So *you* should move.

*   *   *

Yes, this broken-neck
Sleeping position is quite
Popular with us.

CAT HAIKU

Sometimes when I sit
On your lap, I'm a kitten
Again. It will pass.

* * *

You read books; I like
To lie on top of them. We're
Both bibliophiles.

I sleep with one paw
Protecting my nose. You just
Can't be too careful.

Ongoing
Concerns

I watch you use the
Vacuum cleaner but I still
Think it will eat me.

* * *

I figure if I
Stare at this door long enough,
You will let me out.

I hump my back in
Stiff disapproval. One day
I may tell you why.

*　*　*

I hate the garbage
Man. He's noisy and never
Spills anything good.

I sit in front of
The door. You open it; I
Stare. Nope. Changed my mind.

* * *

I'm quiet; you're loud.
I want to play; you want to
Read. And so it goes.

I wasn't really
Waiting for you. No, I just
Happened to be here.

* * *

Delicately, I
Sniff your hand. You've been petting
A strange cat. Traitor!

Small
Amusements

I lick your hand and
Watch you pretend to like it.
This amuses me.

*   *   *

Up in my cat tree
I watch you pass by. Growling,
I jump on your head.

Don't be so crabby.
I'm not 'biting your hair', I'm
Checking you for fleas.

*   *   *

I purr on your lap.
Then I decide I don't know
You. I scratch you hard.

I sit, nose to the
Wall, and stare at it. I know
You'll investigate.

*   *   *

You use dental floss.
So what's wrong with chewing on
Electrical cords?

I like to sniff at
Your feet till you feel odd and
Try to get away.

* * *

You call and I hear.
But I am a jungle cat
And will not answer.

I deign to play with
The string because you look so
Silly dragging it.

*   *   *

Sometimes when I'm bored
I hunch up and look ill just
To make you nervous.

I reach out a claw
And catch a thread in your best
Shirt. It snags; I yawn.

* * *

You have a nightmare.
I fling myself against the
Door to cheer you up.

Secret
Pleasures

I like it when you
Rub just inside my cars. You'd
Make a good Q-Tip.

* * *

It's nice when you scratch
Just above my nose; that's an
Acupressure point.

When I'm pleased, I stick
Out the tip of my tongue. Hey,
We all do SOMEthing.

* * *

Poor you. Only your
Head fits on this expensive
Down pillow? How sad.

I like to rub my
Head against you. Affection?
Nope – my ears just itch.

*   *   *

So I like to stretch
Out with my rump in the air.
It's just a small quirk.

See? The car windshield
Does make an absolutely
Perfect slide for me.

*   *   *

Give me one good reason
Why in heaven's name I should
Not sleep in the sink.

Things I Wonder About

I want out. I want
In. Out. In. Out. In. Out. In.
Are you angry yet?

*   *   *

To help support us
I leave small dead things on the
Doormat. Want some mouse?

You're dashing to work
In the rain. I yawn and stretch —
Don't you just hate me?

* * *

You lie on the couch;
I walk on your stomach. Should
I rest here? Maybe.

Nonchalantly, I
Try to free my claw from your
Shirt. What's so funny?

* * *

You rush, and I weave
Between your legs. You curse; why?
This is my Cat Dance.

Just because I wrecked
The house, you're talking about
Guitar strings? Calm down.

*   *   *

You wash your hands when
You touch my flea collar. Why
Should I *wear* it, then?

What does it feel like
To be big, hairless, tail-less,
And *pink*? Bad, I'll bet.

CAT HAIKU

The Differences
Between Us

Now, wait a minute.
Me, wear a ribbon? You have
Got to be kidding.

* * *

I close my second
Eyelids a lot, just because
You don't have any.

You may have those odd
'Opposable thumbs', but I
Can talk with my tail.

* * *

I land on my feet
For the same reason you walk
Upright: I can. Hah!

You get a massage,
I roll in the dirt. Both are
Relaxing, aren't they?

*   *   *

Come on, admit it.
Don't you sometimes wish *you* had
Sharp little fangs, too?

You play cards; I like
To creep inside paper bags.
To each their own, huh?

* * *

Hey – if I wanted
To walk on the end of a
Leash, I'd be a dog!

You stomp around and
Yell; I lash my tail. There *are*
Other ways to swear.

* * *

Okay, so you blow
Your nose; I rub mine with a
Paw. Who looks cuter?

You do puzzles; I
Unwind viscera from dead
Prey. Hobbies differ.

*   *   *

You laugh, but I know
You wish your yawns swallowed
Up your whole face, too.

You must love this thing
Called 'work' since you go there so
Much. *I'd* rather nap.

* * *

You mean that when you're
Happy, all you can do is
Hum? That's *pathetic*.

Holidays

New Year's Eve is nice
If you're crazy. Me, I stay
Under the sofa.

* * *

You ignore it, but
I'd like to help that groundhog
See his old shadow!

Valentine's Day. Humpf.
I never see candy or
Cards coming *my* way.

* * *

Next St. Patrick's Day,
I'll turn something of *yours* green.
And it won't be food.

CAT HAIKU

Ah, Easter: eggs and
Plastic grass. Now if I could
Just find that Bunny . . .

* * *

There's Mother's Day and
Father's Day, but no Cat Day.
Someone's head should roll.

Fireworks pop until
My eyes do, too. A pox on
Independence Day!

* * *

I won't help with the
Candles, but your birthday cake
Looks quite intriguing . . .

Repeatedly, our
Door opens to loud children.
I loathe Halloween.

* * *

Thanksgiving: there are
No words. A dead bird bigger
Than I am, and cooked!

A tree to climb, light
Cords to bite, presents to prowl.
I *love* Christmastime.

Not-So-Random Thoughts

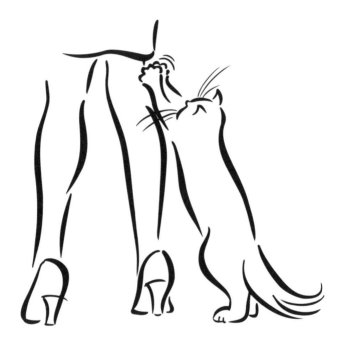

I love pantyhose.
But only when you have just
Put them on for work.

* * *

'There's more than one way
To skin a cat' – what sadist
Thought *that* one up, huh?

If you could see in
The dark like I can, you'd go
Crazy sometimes, too.

* * *

The Cat's Credo: 'All
Creatures Smaller Than You Are
Must Be Played to Death.'

There is no one as
Dignified as we cats; I
Think it's the whiskers.

* * *

A cat getting your
Tongue is impossible; you
Guys are way too tall.

I know I look odd
When I lie on my back, but
Guess what: you do, too.

*   *   *

No matter what you
Give me, I'll shake it in my
Mouth and break its neck.

Cats were revered in
Ancient Egypt. I think we
Should reclaim the past.

*　*　*

You say 'It's raining
Cats and dogs.' *I* wonder what
You've been ingesting.

Please bear in mind that
You're part of *my* entourage,
And not vice versa.

* * *

A bit of advice:
Purring is just a decoy.
Trust me on this one.

Curiosity
May kill us cats, but hey – there
Are worse ways to go!

* * *

I feel no need to
Accomplish things. I exist;
That's triumph enough.

About the Author

Deborah Coates is a chronically amused and frequently perplexed baby boomer who lives in Los Angeles with her two cats, Pinch and Pippin. A native Southern Californian, she is addicted to reading and international travel, and would spend the rest of her days in jeans and Hawaiian shirts if it were left up to her.

Got a cat haiku? Or other comments (preferably
complimentary, but whatever)? Send 'em along to:

cathaiku@hotmail.com

They will be eagerly read and cheerfully responded to –
or at least the nice ones will be.